Creative Solutions Art Book

By
Alice Aida Ayers

TABLE OF CONTENTS

INTRODUCTION

.

This is how my life in Zanzibar began...

So desperate was I to get back to the continent that I didn't realize I had booked my flight ticket to the wrong destination. I was going to the University of Dar es Salaam on a Rotary Ambassadorial Scholarship, located in Dar es Salaam, Tanzania. The plane touched down at a tiny airport surrounded by beautiful coconut trees and the Indian Ocean. I disembarked, collected my bags and stepped into the scorching sun and unbelievable humidity, to be immediately bombarded by men yelling taxi, taxi in my ears.

I chose one and asked to be taken to the University, with a look of total confusion on his face he explained that there was no university on Zanzibar.

"Of course, there must be a university, the University of Dar es Salaam, I exclaimed. He replied, "That's in Dar es Salaam, on the mainland". He suggested that I take a ferry to Dar es Salaam, and kindly helped me to purchase a ticket to the mainland. This is how what be almost 20 years in Zanzibar began, with confusion and misdirection. Who knew that the place where I mistakenly landed was the place I would call home for the next 18 years of my life!

I boarded a ferry and set off to Dar es Salaam. I was so overtaken with exhaustion and jet lag that I made it on automatic pilot, trusting that the universe would guide me. After checking into the university and being assigned a dorm room, I slept for 16 hours!

Over the next two months, the registration process would prove to be complicated and less than transparent. I had become quite frustrated with the university system in Dar. I felt that I had been lured there under false pretenses, it turned out that the program I had signed up for did not exist. I soon lost patience and decided to take a weekend break in Zanzibar. Upon my return to Dar I made the decision that the university was not the place for me.

The Seduction of Zanzibar

After having spent 2 months on campus and not being able to achieve anything, my desire to continue waned. I packed my bags, did not bother checking out of the dorm and returned to the island.

Deciding to stay in Zanzibar and not return to Dar was easy. Zanzibar has a way of seducing your senses and lures one into wanting to be a part of it. I checked into the Hotel Kiponda where another Rotary scholar was staying and I immediately felt at home. Island life had never really appealed to me as such, but as I said, this island was seductive.

My room at Kiponda was on the ground floor near the staff workspace, I made new friends with the housekeepers. The months passed so quickly, my days were filled with attending classes at the Swahili Institute, touring the island, swimming, making art and hanging out with the hotel staff. My meals were taken with the staff where I was indoctrinated in Swahili culture and food. I absolutely loved it! I spent many hours talking with the man who eventually became my partner.

Two other Rotary scholars from America joined me in Zanzibar one weekend and we took a taxi to tour the slave chamber in Mangapwani village.

I remember speaking the words, "I could live here".

As we were driven through the village with its enormous mango trees and the smell of jasmine in the air, I remember speaking the words, "I could live here". There was something mystical that grabbed at my soul, a sense of familiarity I couldn't quite place, it went beyond the physical beauty, it was almost mystical. It felt more like a memory. We visited the areas where people who had been forced into slavery were housed until they got shipped out. I was overwhelmed with emotion when I entered the underground chamber and I felt the energies of those ancestors pulling at me. When I left the village that day, I knew a part of me had stayed behind.

Creative Solutions

The years I spent as project manager for Creative Solutions Resource Systems on the island of Zanzibar taught me more lessons than I could have ever imagined. Lessons came to me on life, love, art, process, patience and appreciation. Lessons come in so many ways and in so many forms as you go through life. For me those that come from making art and teaching art are the most profound. Because I feel those lessons have been so instrumental to my growth, I have a need to share them. I put together this book of projects, the processes and techniques, as well as the life lessons learnt on this beautiful, sometimes frustrating journey. Living in the country of Tanzania, on the island of Zanzibar is akin to living in an art studio. There is so much inspiration, color, texture and harmony in nature and the people. The Creative Solutions project that I created was a humming, living art workshop happening every day. The following pages are filled with images of the art that came out of my love for the project and the place that was my home for over 18 years. It was based on the following principles, which I still hold in my heart.

Values I hold in my heart:

Creativity
The belief in finding solutions creatively. The willingness to try things in the community, in order to address an unmet need.

Respectability
Treating every person with respect and being aware of the dignity of each person encountered.

Encouragement
Standing beside those being served, and encouraging self-sustainability, growth and capacity building.

Attentive
Serving the community and being open and flexible to change based on the needs of the community.

Tenacity
Being determined to bring the best one has to offer to a project. Never giving up on the people working and the people served.

Integrity
High priority is placed on living out these principles – in relationships, programs and organizational practices.

Versatility
Being open to new ideas, especially ideas from those being served, and seeking ways to create flexible, user-friendly services.

Empathy
Listening, encouraging, getting to know the community, providing help and guidance, and advocating in a spirit of kindness and compassion.

Project 1: brick making

clay and mud bricks

In the village of Mangapwani and many others in Tanzania, clay and mud bricks are a traditional material used in building houses. Prior to cement and sand for the making of bricks, everyone used this process for building.

...creating connection and allowing communication with the ancestors.

For me, the desire to create environmentally friendly objects and art takes on new meaning in Africa. There is a special magic that occurs when you dig into the dirt, pour water on it and knead it. In many ways digging into the earth and building with earth has a certain ancestral nostalgia attached to it.

It places us in a familial space, creating a connection and allowing for communion with the ancestors. In this village, there were still many people who chose to use this method of building as opposed to cement bricks. Not only is it more budget friendly, it also keeps the interior cool, the need for fans and air conditioning is not necessary.

One must be willing to work for many hours in the sun in order to pull together a project. Making bricks is difficult and fun! It begins with digging sand and digging dirt, then mixing those together with water. Frames for the bricks are made from wood that is nailed into rectangular shapes, approximately 3" by 8".

When the mixture reaches the consistency of a heavy paste, it is ready to pour. The mud mixture is poured into the forms, packed in using a board or piece of wood, then set in the sun to dry. After one to two weeks of drying the bricks are ready for use. Using the same mud mixture as mortar, the bricks are used in a in a brick laying manner, that is one row on the bottom with 2 inches in between, the second row staggered as to reach half on each bottom brick. This method of stacking bricks strengthens the structure.

In this case, we built a kiln which was used to melt glass! After the bricks are laid, a coat of mortar mixture is applied by rubbing it over the surface of the structure; it is left to cure for a few weeks before fire is used.

Project 2: slumping glass

possibilities for recycling

I came up with the idea to work with glass bottles in 2011. Prior to that I had been teaching computers and English, it took me four years and hundreds of hours to raise enough money to buy 12 laptop computers and fit the library with enough solar power to run them.

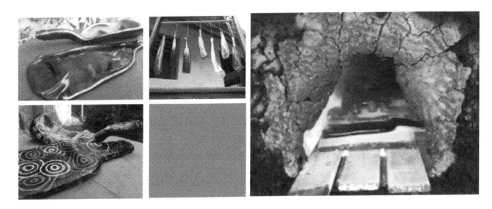

I contacted sponsors and literally carried some of the computers from the US all the way back to Zanzibar. The new enrollment was up to 30 students and we had just finished a four-month semester of computer training. Ramadhan was just ending and it was time for a break as the Eid celebrations were beginning. I said my goodbyes to the last of the students and retired to my room. When I rose the next day I went to the library to discover that all the computers were gone! I walked out into the courtyard to see that the solar panels from the roof were also missing. Some skillful thieves had come through during the midnight hours and wiped us out.

I kept thinking, I can't do this anymore! All those hours, months of work to get the computers a solar equipment, gone in a single night. I was so distraught, I went for a walk on the beach to try and relax. During my walk, I cut my foot on a piece of broken glass. I didn't know at the time, this had a purpose.

The rubbish created by hotels always bothered me so I put out a notice to hotels and individuals to bring me their bottles. I acquired thousands of glass bottles and began researching the internet for ways to recycle. I had seen slumped bottles and was fascinated with the transformation of the bottle. Not having worked with glass before was a little intimidating but I was determined to learn and I had a few thousand bottles to play with. After several attempts with the wood-burning kiln I succeeded. I am not sure if it was more thrilling to see the fire reach the temperatures required, to see the bottles slowly droop and lay into the form or to hold the finished piece. All I can say is that there is a primal emotion which is evoked through the combination of glass and fire. The beautiful thing is to see how uniquely each piece evolves. Sometimes the most beautiful unexpected object materializes, it really is magic!

Getting to the point at which the bottle is kiln ready is not an immediate process.

Bottle Slumping Process

1. The bottles must be soaked and cleaned, preferably in hot water, if there is no hot water available then soak for a couple of days. The labels and excess glue are removed (scrape with a knife if necessary) and the bottle is washed thoroughly.

2. The surface on which the bottle will be placed in the kin must be prepared with a separator like kiln wash, we used kaolin mixed with water and painted the molds and other surfaces. When using kiln wash, be sure the surface is very smooth. Any brush strokes, bumps, etc. will show up in the glass.

3. When loading the kiln, make sure there is room for the bottles to expand without touching. In using the homemade brick kiln, we loaded the firewood and started it off very slowly. Too big a flame too soon will cause the bottle to crack. Set fire at about 100 C for one hour then slowly increase the temperature every 30 minutes until it reaches full flame, approximately 900C.

4. After the bottle starts to slump, the fire can be allowed to burn out slowly over a 24-hour period. The following day the items are ready for removal.

Project 3: mosaic murals

"I hear and I forget, I see and I remember, I do and I understand." –Confucius

I developed a reputation as a recycler and people began bringing all of sorts of projects, bottle caps, broken tile and plastic. It was overwhelming for me at times and the students of Creative Solutions thought that I had lost my mind.

I teach from a very experiential perspective, having people involve themselves in every process.

Creative Solutions became an "Experiential Learning Centre" in 2010, rooted in the philosophy of holistic and experiential learning. The program was divided into three phases—Explore, Understand, and Create.

The **Explore phase** transpired through games, discussions, and hands-on activities, ensuring that activities are fun, engaging, and socially relevant.

Environmental education is one of the cornerstones of the CSRS. Participants are presented with issues which will serve as a theme throughout the program.

Themes include solid waste management, composting, recycling, gardening, natural resource management. Participants are encouraged to explore how these issues and themes affect them as individuals and their local communities.

The **Understand phase** of the program allows participants to take an in-depth look at how things work.

Processes such as solar energy, compost gardening, recycling, and glasswork allow participants to understand the impact of our daily actions on the environment. Participants have the opportunity to ask questions, learn new vocabulary, and ultimately tie in their experiences with lessons in school such as biology, chemistry, physics, art, and language.

In the **Create phase**, students use art to come up with solutions to the issues presented to them in the Explore phase. Art is at the heart of activities at Creative Solutions.

The art activities include:

- mosaic/murals, upcycled art
- theatre/performance
- music
- paper making
- puppet making
- glass art
- dance and movement

Mosaic murals not only became a solution for how to use the excessive materials on hand, it also became a way to create long lasting, sustainable beauty. It is such a rewarding process, similar to creating a puzzle, fitting each piece in its space and watching an image emerge. After visits from organizations such as ACRA of Italy, Save The Children and Zanzibar International Film Festival (ZIFF, we were commissioned to teach the process and create mosaic murals in schools in Stone Town and around the island. An art contest was held in 8 secondary schools in the Stone Town.

Out of over one thousand drawings, I created a composite which expressed the most relevant images the children had come up with. Myself and two of the CSRS staff distributed the sketch to the schools and my team and I visited the students who would be involved and taught them the process of making mosaic art. I used images from books to explain the history of mosaic and how it was used in mosques for centuries. Those conservative students in the group felt more comfortable when they learned this fact. The children, between ages 13 to 17, took to the process easily and excitedly, having never seen nor tried anything like this before. The children from each school brought discarded items from around their homes to incorporate in the murals. We completed eight 4 ft x 8 ft murals in one month. Each based on the same drawing, all absolutely original and different. Upon returning to the compound I continued to create my own mosaic murals and to teach as many villagers as possible to do the same. My goal was to fill every empty wall with color and lyrical images that welcomed you into a wonderland of love and bliss.

I applied for, and received money to create a project for schools around the island. Over one year, 20 schools came to the compound on field trips. There were 20 children per group from age 8 to 17 and they spent the day creating art. They learned to cut bottles, make handmade paper from scraps, create puppets from plastic bottles and scraps, and they learned to mosaic!

Instructions for Mosaic Art

1. *Pick the base to use for your design.* You can create a mosaic on almost any surface. It should be strong enough to handle the weight of your mosaic pieces and the glue and grout. Tables, planters, bird baths, or walking stones are all great options

2. *Choose the materials you want to use to make your mosaic.* Materials include glass, stones, tiles, seashells, or anything else you can find.

3. *Draw your design on the base.* Use a pencil to sketch your image.

4. *Lay your mosaic pieces over your design before gluing them down.* Arrange the pieces how you'd like and preview how they will look before you glue them on. Clean dirt or debris before laying them out.

5. *Choose the right adhesive for the materials you are using.* Depending on the materials you can use acrylic based adhesives, epoxy resins, or construction adhesives.

6. *Arrange the mosaic pieces on top of your design.* Spread the adhesive on the surface and apply tiles starting in one corner of the design and work across in rows. Make sure the gaps between the tiles are about $\frac{1}{8}$ inch or less.

7. *Let the adhesive set.* The time needed varies depending on the type of adhesive you used and where your mosaic will be, so check the label on your adhesive and follow the directions stated there.

8. *Apply the grout using a spatula.* Lay newspaper down on your work surface and place the mosaic on it. Cover the whole mosaic with grout, spreading it with a spatula and filling in the creases between the tiles

9. *Let the grout set and wipe away the excess.* Let the grout set for about 20 minutes, then wipe clean.

Project 4: puppet making

karagosi

This project was initiated by Mr. Issac Bablo when he visited the compound. He is an amazing theatre director and wanted to interpret one of his plays to incorporate singing puppets. He grew up in Zanzibar before the revolution and one of his fondest memories was going to Mnazi Mmoja park in town to watch the puppet shows. In Swahili they are called "karagosi".

He asked me if I could create some characters, I happily obliged and together with the students we created puppets from recycled plastic, newspaper and glue. A lovely woman named Lucy, taught Paper Mache puppet making classes for several weeks and also created the most amazing animal puppets imaginable.

Issac spent a few weeks teaching our acting group the script and defining the characters for the play. They really excelled. The puppets took on lives of their own and we all bonded with these inanimate objects as we brought them to life. We performed at the film festival in town and travelled to villages around the island, performing for sold out crowds. Issac said he felt like he was back in his childhood watching the shows during the big "Sikuku" (big holidays) in Zanzibar.

Over the following months after Issac left, we developed scripts that were geared toward the village people specifically using puppet theater to address social ills and abuse. We wrote about the tradition of pregnant women using unqualified "Mganga" or healers to address pregnancy complications, environmental issues such as deforestation and litter, and we addressed child sexual abuse and early marriage taking place in the village. It was risky but through the puppets women and young girls were able to tell their stories and receive much needed help and guidance.

One of the nicest compliments I received came from an amazing puppeteer from Germany. It cemented the fact that when your work has a purpose, it turns it into play. The only difference between work and play is the reason that you do it.

*"Meeting **Aida Ayers** in Africa, 9000 km from Germany, deeply impressed me. Not only was it a fantastic experience to see her works of art in the tropical environment and to watch her remarkable activities for culture and self-sustainability in her new home country. She moreover reminded me of my own theatre project I founded back home in Berlin, 20 years ago. I also established a place of art and culture, up to this very day to me and many others have a magic place of theatre play, of beauty, self-sustained culture and encouragement to young and old. The power to achieve this in many years of hard work and financial insecurity I have drawn from the fascination to find a meaningful life with creative work, and to pass this energy on to others. Experiencing **Aida Ayers'** project and her own strong and vital personality has given me new energy to continue my own work and to continue my own search for creative solutions". – Thomas Mierau, March 2013-03-13*

Project 5: glass appliqué

similar to stained glass

Prior to learning the process making of stained glass, I discovered a process called glass applique. It is a very simple and fulfilling technique. The end result looks similar to stained glass, but it is a fraction of the cost to create. It requires using a piece of float glass or window glass as a foundation for the project.

Similar to stained glass, the equipment required is the same up to the point of putting it together as a cohesive work of art. You will need glass cutting tools, sanding equipment or sand paper, measuring tools and drawing materials. I recommend the following link to learn more about traditional stained-glass equipment and process.

You can either create your own patterns or choose from the thousands available on line. After the pieces of glass are cut to the right proportions, you will apply them with a clear glue and leave to dry overnight or longer depending on how humid it is. In Zanzibar, the humidity sometimes prevented projects from drying in a timely manner. After the pieces are adhered to the clear glass surface and remaining glue is cleaned, the next step of grouting is completed.

After creating so many grand mosaic murals, grouting became second nature. The glass applique' piece is grouted in the same way, filing in spaces and smoothing the surface, finally wiping it off after it has dried. The result is a beautiful image, which closely resembles stained glass. While this is in no way a replacement for the magical process of creating stained glass, it is an easier and inexpensive alternative to the real thing. The students were thrilled and for some who had tried the actual stained-glass process, the applique was less frustrating for them. The following pieces were installed as windows and glowed as beautifully from the inside and from outside of the hand-built bottle house that they still adorn.

Instructions for Stained Glass Applique

1 Design

· Cut out the glass for your design to be glued to an ordinary window glass.
· The edges of the stained-glass pieces should be sanded or grinded and glued to the window glass.

2 Attaching the Glass

· There are several different types of glue which can be used to adhere glass to glass. I have used Weldbond, Araldite, and other clear and white adhesives.
· Glues must be spread evenly and in thin coats.
· Allow the glued pieces to dry for a couple of weeks before grouting the seams.

3 Grouting

· Grout is available in a variety of colors, but all are opaque and appear black in a back-lit panel in a window or light-box.
· Follow the instructions on the package and let it thicken a bit before you begin to spread it on the surface.
· do not add too much water to the mixture.

4 Cleaning the finished piece

· The finished piece will have grout smeared on the surface, do not be alarmed.
· After grouting the entire surface, it should stand for five to ten minutes.
· Gently wipe the surface with damp towels, this will clean off most of the grout residue.
· Let it stand overnight and remove any remainder of grout from the stained glass surfaces with steel wool.

Special Project: mr. boom boom

A volunteer and friend, Rachel and I had already begun a project to reduce plastic waste and batteries, Creative Solutions received a donation of 10,000 bottles. We were building a sculpture in which we had stuffed kilos of non-perishable trash. We named him Mr. BoomBoom because his behind was huge. Rachel created his enormous legs out of tin cans and his arms were made from plastic trash wrapped in chicken wire then coated in cement, later the entire sculpture was covered in mosaic with recycled bottle caps. He was a looker too! Rachel and I had been to town where we purchased some artifacts from an old man. He was stricken with gout and his legs were huge, the image would not leave Rachel's head, and Mr. BoomBoom was fashioned to pay homage to him. This project was developed for our Stone Town students. I wanted them to be exposed to other materials available on the island, to have a lesson in sculpture and to get away from the tourist circuit by spending a week in the village. We started out with 6 students and wound up with four. Each of them contributed to the design of the piece and we combined the ideas into a cohesive model. It was complete in about two weeks and all those who've seen it have enjoyed it!

Project 6: bottle house

"the boomboom room"

So what do you do when you have 5000 bottles lying around the yard? You build a bottle house of course! I had no idea how, but I knew what I wanted. We were just finishing up the sculpture, Mr. Boom Boom when I had the great idea of building the house around him. Two walls already existed and I calculated it would take about 3 months to get it finished.

The three-month project was finally complete 13 months later! But it turned out beautifully. Building with bottles is challenging. We used cement and sand as mortar after first trying dirt and realizing that it would not adhere to the bottles during rainy season. There were a lot of false starts with this project and trying to get the students interested proved to be more difficult that I had anticipated. For the most part, they felt that it was a waste of time, it was too different and too much work. And it definitely was more work than I had thought it would be. It proved to be a lesson in not giving up. I had a dream and I was not about to let it go.

I ended up bribing my guys with food and extra time off. It was worth the hassle it took to get it done. And in the meantime, whenever I was hosting a group of students from abroad, they were more than happy to add to the construction and the finishing of the Boom Boom Room! As with all construction , a strong base is essential. We used bricks and cement. The sizes of the bottles varied, this was not the best choice, it is better to have similar size and shaped bottles for a more cohesive construction. But the colored bottles looked so pretty, I couldn't resist. As with the fences which had been built previously, the house held up firmly against the elements. The floor was the last thing to go in and it too was mosaiced and filled with crushed glass.

I would spend hours using it as a meditation room, cleaning the glass art it eventually held and hiding in it when I was too tired to do anything else. But ultimately, it was a work of art that people, both locally and from abroad, had heard of and would come to see. It presented new ideas for recycling. For Zanzibari people, it opened their eyes to the beauty of glass bottles and the possibilities.

Project 7: fused glass

I must credit the internet with being my teacher in glass fusing. I had no idea how to create fused glass so I researched it and experimented a lot. All of wonderful mistakes turned out to be an amazing education in glass fusing! I acquired an electric kiln from a friend who was leaving the island, but it came with no instructions and a couple of parts missing. Again the internet proved to be a valuable resource. I got the kiln working and we started putting glass together and fusing. The items we created were a big hit at craft fairs and we also held classes for outsiders for a fee which contributed nicely to our bottom line. The small glass pieces were cut and assembled by the students then loaded in the kiln and I was responsible for the firing. With my kiln it took approximately 3.5 hours for the firing to be complete, then I let it coo down until the following morning. The glass used was from recycled bottles, broken window glass and scraps of colored glass we collected from glass shops in town.

Project 8: bottle cutting

I experimented with several ways of cutting bottles. I googled and watched YouTube videos. I tried soaking a string in kerosene, wrapping around the bottle lighting it on fire. This method did not work and proved to be dangerous. I finally discovered a tool called the G-2 which I found was easy to assemble and convenient to use. Instructions for bottle cutting can be found on line at

www.diamondcrafs.com

Project 9: wind chimes

There is something so divine about the sound of the glass tinkling as the ocean breeze blows it softly. I had seen images of chimes made with a halved top portion of a bottle, so that's where I began, they were beautiful, but soon I wanted more of that beautiful sound. I wanted more drama, so I began creating wind chimes with multiple strings of glass. I learned to cut rings from wine and beer bottles and began slumping those. I soon discovered that each type bottle created a different sound, even after the glass rings were slumped and their edges smooth, not to mention how incredibly beautiful they looked when they glistened in the sun. Theses chimes quickly became a favorite at art markets on the island and in Dar es Salaam. We sold hundreds of them and the money went to increase staff salaries and teach the outreach classes. It seemed like I could not walk into a restaurant or shop that didn't have at least one of Creative Solution's chimes hanging and tinging! This obsession soon led to the creating of chandeliers.

"Listen,' she whispered and pointed towards the window. 'Whenever the wind blows from the east and the wind chimes dance in the moonlight, there is magic in the air."
Author: Carole Carlton

Project 10: chandeliers

I love transforming bottles

The light, when it shines through colored glass, glistens in my soul. I love glass. I also love transforming bottles, broken glass and glass scraps into other objects. I taught myself to cut, slump and melt glass into shapes and molds. Soon I wanted to see how far I could push my own creativity. Not having access to the resources from the internet, I had to rely on a lot of experimenting and suggestions from other artists and visitors. On a trip to Italy, I found glass paint which was made in Germany, it was perfect for creating more colorful glass. The chandeliers were of such a variety, some with different shapes, some with over 200 glass rings cut and slumped from wine bottles. I quickly became obsessed with the crazy, yet beautiful art that came about.

Project 11: glass bottle tiles

After cutting the glass bottles and using parts to make windchimes, drinking glasses and containers, I ended up with a lot of scrap. One day I slumped some of these middle sections in the kiln and discovered the most beautiful tiles! Yes! A new project. I slumped top halves and bottoms and I had a new obsession. I decided I was going to tile my entire house with these gorgeous tiles. I cut them and shaped them and began attaching to my house. I got one of my art students to assist and he loved it too! With so many bottles on the premises, I had to keep coming up with ideas on how to use them. I tried making stepping stones, built the wall around the premises, the bottle house and still the resource of bottles was exhaustive. To me, this was pure joy, it meant that I would not run out of my art supplies. But the tiles were by far one of the most amazing uses of scrap glass. The house began looking like something out of a fairy tale.

Project 12: outdoor sculpture

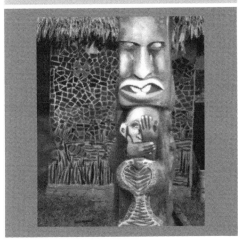

Creating sculpture is especially challenging in Zanzibar. Being an island in which 95% of the population is Muslim presents issues with how sculpture is executed. This means that for many, the belief that anything representing a living being cannot be painted, sculpted, drawn or created. It took me many years of teaching classes in art education to help people understand that we were not creating art for the sake of worship. We were creating it because of the educational benefits, the critical thinking skills that were gained from making art and the very need to express oneself in a creative atmosphere, whether it was representing a figure or a geometrical design. Some of the sculptures in the images were created together with students of Creative Solutions and several of them went on to become artists in their own right.

The bottle tree is possibly my favorite of all sculptures. There were many hands involved in its execution, but the design was mine. Prior to making Zanzibar my home, I was working on my doctorate in Art Education and for my dissertation I wrote about art of the African Diaspora.

One aspect that fascinated me most was the spiritual beliefs that had spread across the diaspora, among them was the belief that a bad spirit or 'jinn' could be captured and contained in a bottle hanging from a tree. Hence the development of the bottle tree, and somehow, I believe that I was protected from spirits sent to harm me. The base was constructed of cement blocks that were shaped and the corners rounded to create a cylinder. After it was cemented together, holes were drilled to insert the branches. Over the years the branches broke, as they were originally constructed from old tree branches. I eventually replaced them with branches made from metal wrapped in fabric the cemented. I replaced bottles that broke or when I developed new bottle designs. Each side presents a different feature made from a combination of mosaic, bottle caps, painted and sculpted images and found objects. As the bottle caps became worn they developed a patina finish, the tree became more beautiful and sacred to me

Project 13: mural painting

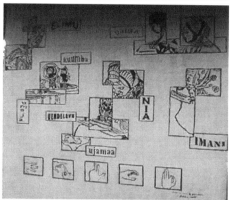

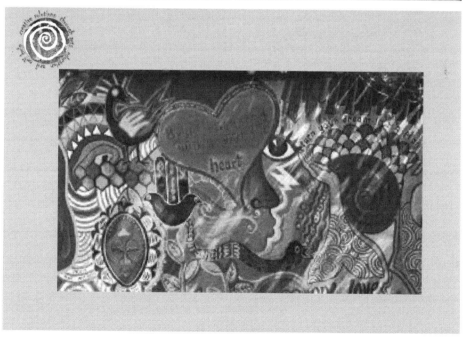

By the time I reached my 10th year on the island, I was desperate to have some good permanent paint for murals and my personal work. I had spent many years making my own paint from lime wash and powdered pigment. The islands which make up Zanzibar are formed out of a base of limestone from which buildings, homes and roads were built. It can also be transformed into a powder and used to paint. I painted murals, pictures and my house inside and out with paint I made from limestone. Making this paint is hard work and the colors are not strong, and since it was a wash it was not permanent. The only other paint available on the island was an enamel which was for painting cars. I decided to bring paint with me from America each time I visited and I asked friends and volunteers to bring paint with them. Soon we had a supply of acrylics and oils. The murals took on a new life, vibrant and permanent. I designed the majority of the murals and either painted or was a part of all of the paintings. In addition to wanting the place to look beautiful, it was so important for people to absorb the messages within these beautiful works of art. They are filled with messages of gratitude, faith, and inspiration. I remember one of my students calling me a "konokono", which is a snail. He said I leave a trail of paint everywhere I go. I love that and it is truth!

Project 14: puppet theatre

I decided to take puppet making to the community. In Zanzibar, the community is a mix of ex-patriots and local people. Each year I held a summer art camp for the children of this segment of society. Throughout the year, our local students enjoyed all of the benefits of these projects. The summer camp was an opportunity for children from the international schools to get involved.

This project consisted of several parts;

After a session of storytelling to stimulate the imagination, each child created a character. They could choose a person, an animal or a fictional creature to develop. Together we developed and wrote a story based upon the characters they created and we told the story of how they related to one another. This story was turned into a script, in which each child had lines and actions to learn and practice. Puppets were then made from papier Mache', they were painted and costumed. We built and painted a set, rehearsed the play and finally performed for their parents and the community. The process is always so important, especially when young people want to talk but are unable to express themselves in front of others. Puppet theatre is an amazing way for those voices to be heard. I witnessed a shy boy who was in the shadow of his older siblings emerge and become the hero of the story. As with our community puppet theatre, we encouraged the children to talk about issues through their puppets that they could not or would not speak of otherwise. It is so important for our young people to feel that they have a voice!

43

Papier Mache' Recipe

Ingredients

- flour
- water
- mixing bowl
- spoon
- balloon

Activity

Mix one part flour with one part of water (1 cup flour and 1 cup water) until you get a thick glue-like consistency. Add a bit more water if it's too thick.

Mix well with a spoon to get rid of all the lumps. If you find you are getting lumps in your glue, you can use a small kitchen electric mixer to whiz them out.

Add a few tablespoons of salt to the final mixture to help prevent mold.

NOTES:

- You need to use strips of newspaper only, or even paper tissues or paper towels.
- Let the newspaper strips soak in the paper Mache glue a little before using.
- Cover your balloon with only 2-3 layers, then let dry completely. This is an important step.
- Once a layer is dry you can add 2-3 more layers, remembering to let each layer dry before adding the next one.
- The final layer can be plain paper - so it's easier to paint - but use the thinnest paper possible and make sure it's soaked well in the Paper Mache' glue.

https://www.kidspot.com.au

Project 15: handmade paper

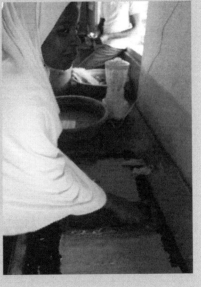

When I proposed to the students that we would make our own paper from brown banana leaves, recyclable trash like old newspaper, kapok tree cotton fibers, flower pedals and old leaves, they looked very confused. I explained that the process was more science than art, and this felt more comfortable to them. Students in Zanzibar were taught theory for most of their educational career, and very seldom did they experience or perform a scientific or artistic experiment. Making paper covered both topics. The leaves and other materials from the trees are soaked overnight in a mixture of Hydrochloric acid and water then rinsed thoroughly.

The following day these materials are put together with small fragments of paper, put in a blender and mixed until it becomes pulp.

The excitement on the faces of the students was invigorating. I loved seeing them make their paper into sheets and carefully place it in the sun to dry. I found myself reminiscing about my university days so many years before when I learned to do this art form and how it made me feel seeing it come together. To be able to share what one learns with others who would possibly never have the opportunity otherwise, is a great gift.

1. Materials You Need:

1. A large bowl
2. Old newspaper, office paper, scraps
3. Water
4. A mixer, food processor or pestle and mortar
5. Two wooden frames 8"-12" (you can buy a standard frame or make one)
6. A screen that's used in a window
7. A stapler or small nails and hammer
8. A large Tub (dishpan for instance)
9. Cloth
10. An iron
11. Optional, dryer Lint, thread, glitter, flowers, thin leaves, pine needles

2. Soak It

To begin, shred the paper into small squares about 1 inch and put them into the bowl with hot water. Let soak for half an hour.

3. Make A Mold

While the paper is soaking, make the mold
Attach the screen to each frame using staples
Leave the other frame blank.
(You can also make molds from screens, or other objects (see below)

4. Turn It Into Pulp

Place the soaked paper in the mixer bowl or food processor half filled with water. Mix at half speed until smooth
-At this point, you can also add small quantities of vegetables or plants to the pulp. In this case, mix until the mixture is uniform. (Only a small amount should be used or you will end up with mush)
-To add color to the paper , add nontoxic fabric dye or food coloring to the mixture.

5. Swish It In a Tub

Pour warm water into the tub until it is half full. Then, pour the pulp into the tub until the mixture resembles thick soup. The thicker the mixture, the thicker your paper will be. Place the frame in and Shake it from side to side to distribute the pulp evenly until it makes a sheet of paper.

6. Drain, Place It In a Mold

Take the paper pulp and frame out of the tub. The other border frame on top. Hold both frames and turn the paper 180 degrees on to the clean frame.

7. Let It Dry

Place the frames horizontally and let it drip dry, or turn it over onto a cloth to dry

8. Iron It

Place another cloth on top. Dry the paper by ironing firmly.
Remove the cloth or letting it dry naturally

9. Using Other Kinds of Molds

You can try other ideas like using baking molds, plastic, plaster or candy molds. This can be fun for ornaments, small gift tags, or wall ornaments. Spray the mold with PAM. Place the damp paper into a mold and let it dry-it should lift out when dry. To hang it add a string while it is wet. *this may take practice.

10. Left Overs

When you are done, you can throw away the screened pulp or keep the drained, leftover pulp in the freezer, in a plastic bag, for later use. NOTE: Do not pour the pulp into the sink or toilet because the pulp could block the drain.

Project 16: community well

Collaboration is key to successful community operations. Whether it is between government, community members or international volunteers. Working together for the greater good is beneficial to all. The well building project was the answer to a crisis in the village. We had not had clean water for several months, so I reached to several organizations for help. One organization which was traveling the continent building wells responded. I had read an article about Roadmonkey Adventure Philanthropy in Oprah Winfreys', O magazine. This was a tour company which also raised funds to help communities in the countries where they travelled. Collaboration between the philanthropic organization, community leaders and Creative Solutions Zanzibar resulted in the building of a well that continues to provide water to over 5000 residents.

Project 17: children's playground

The definition of happiness is seeing children smile, hearing their laughter, and sharing in their joy. The pre-school at Creative Solutions had been active for eight years. Playtime consisted of them running around the compound and playing games the teachers created for them. After a trip to the US during which I saw children climbing on bars, swinging and crawling, I felt that our children needed that type of activity for their bodies and spirits. By that time, I had been active in recycling and re-purposing materials. After a beach clean-up, I had in my possession; tires, a plastic pipe from a well, assorted useable materials, bottle caps, tiles and rope. I started with a swing and a seesaw, then encouraged the staff and volunteers to create anything the children could climb over, under and through!

Project 18: cement Pots

Setting up this community learning initiative was not without its challenges. I was the first foreigner interested in creating a project in Mangapwani village and I was met with a lot of resistance. I was informed by the elders of the village that I could not build a bar or a church. I explained that I was an artist and interested in teaching life skills through the arts. I am sure they had no idea what I was talking about, but I assured them that neither a church nor a bar were on the agenda. Upon getting approval from the village committee, the first people I reached out to were women.

The purpose of this women's initiative was to teach income generation projects as most of them were stay at home mothers, had minimal education, and earned no income of their own. I chose to teach techniques which could be used for more than just making art objects. The first of these projects were cement flower pots which were either painted or mosaiced then sold to hotels and private people. But the lesson was on how to prepare cement and apply it to a surface.

Instructions for Cement pots

Using Ready mix cement, mix equal parts of cement and water. Stir until it is smooth. Two cups will make one medium sized bowl. The mixture should be slightly stiff, not too watery.

Molds can be most materials., plastic bowls works well. Spray your molds, in this case the larger bowl with nonstick cooking spray or any type of oi, and the bottom of the smaller bowl.

Wear gloves and scoop the mixture into the bowl with your hands. Press down and around the sides.

Place the smaller bowl on top of the cement mixture. Place rocks inside to weigh it down.

Let it dry like that for 24 hours, then remove the top bowl using a flathead screwdriver or something to lift it off. Leave the cement piece to harden for a few extra days before painting or applying mosaic tiles.

Once the bottom is removed and the bowl is out of the mold, sand the edges.

Drill holes in the bottom of the bowl for drainage

Project 19: wooden spoons

I became obsessed with wooden spoons after seeing the variety of shapes and sizes at the market one day. For me the spoon represents nourishment, sustenance and care. I used it as a metaphor for women. We share all the same qualities. I envisioned the spoon as a woman preparing meals for her family, feeding those are hungry and being strong to be of utilitarian use. It was interesting to me how men carved these spoons from a single piece of wood with such care and love. I became collecting the wooden spoons and recreating them as works of art representing some form of femininity. I carved and shaped some of spoons, attached found objects and painted them. In the end I recreated 100 spoons and had an exhibition entitled 'Miko Mia', One Hundred Wooden Spoons. The show explored traditional and contemporary roles of women in various cultures.

Project 20: brick donations

While building the classroom, I ran out of funds and had to be creative to raise money for its completion. Fundraising is always challenging, writing proposals is not my strong point so most of our funding came from personal relationships. I tried numerous times to apply for funding from embassies and philanthropic organizations but to no avail. I made connections with business people in Zanzibar and started to promote CSRS to local organizations. Small donations started coming in and we were able to build our classroom.

We literally built the classroom 50,000 shillings at a time. I started a fundraiser where I sold a brick for that amount and with the money we purchased building materials. People would tell me what they wanted on their brick, colors to used or logos and I started creating them. I designed and painted, mosaiced and sculpted over 100 bricks. At some point it became fashionable for people to come and paint their own bricks.

Project 21: bottle painting

With so many bottles available from hotels, I was challenged to find creative ways of using them. Sometimes, it is necessary just to use them as a canvas. I used acrylic paint and varnished them after they dried. To create fine lines, I recycled plastic squeeze bottles with a tip and filled them with paint. Other bottles were mosaiced with beads and old glass or tiles. A heavy glue which dries clear can be used to adhere the objects.

Some of the bottles became bird feeders, others flower holder and candle holders. Some were used to hang and admire. This is a relaxing way to reuse and give a new life to an old bottle.

Project 22: painted furniture

I began painting furniture in the late 1970's when I found a discarded chair on the street. I couldn't afford to purchase any furniture at the time but I had paints! I developed a passion for painting wooden tables, chairs and cabinets. This passion only increased for the decades and I continued doing so at the center and encouraging others to reuse and redesign their old pieces into beautiful, useable works of art. These tables were commissioned pieces. I used acrylic paint and finished them with a few coats of varnish. When applying the varnish it is important to allow each coat to dry thoroughly to achieve a smooth finish. These tables are over ten years old and still look fresh and beautiful. The images reflect my connection with West African symbolism, Eastern philosophy and East African fabric design.

Project 23: quilting and applique

My mother was a quilter and my grandmother created appliqué pieces. So quilting held an interest for me. I enjoyed looking at traditional quilts, however I was not interested in creating them, that is until I viewed an exhibition of contemporary quilting by the brilliant artist Faith Ringgold. It inspired me to make some of my own and subsequently start a quilting class. I love working with textiles and I love the beautiful fabrics from the African continent. I was already creating batik and painting fabric so I combined what I knew and played further. After putting a piece together I loved to applique and embellish with whatever objects I have available. This is very much in the tradition of West African textile artists. I use beads, threads, shells, even discarded colorful plastic to turn the textile into relief art. Relief is a sculptural technique where the elements remain attached to a solid background. The term relief is means to raise. The attached materials have been raised above the background plane.

Project 24: stained glass

I had explored and thoroughly enjoyed working with glass applique, but I really wanted to learn the art of stained glass. On a visit to the US one year I decided to take a course to learn the mysteries of stained glass. I always loved working with solder and had the opportunity to learn how to use the medium while working with electricity. But this was really special. I already knew how to cut glass and sand it with regular sand paper, but not how to use the other tools involved. The course paid off and I returned with a new class in stained glass. Because we did not have a large supply of stained glass or access to solder, the projects were small. I acquired the equipment and we used the copper foil method. We created angels, dragonflies and small windows that we could sell at the annual holiday fairs. The students took to using this media so effortlessly, it soon became a favorite.

Project 25:
Products

My dream was to create a community organization which would serve the needs of villagers and inspire through art and education. The project exceeded my goals. The number of people that went on to higher education, were able to support their families and developed an understanding of how art serves humanity was much greater than I had thought it would be. Below are some of the items that we created and sold and it was through those sales that the center became self-sustaining and provided income and a better quality of life for thousands of residents. Perhaps this book will continue to inspire others to be creative and appreciate the value of arts education. The benefits of creating art and learning through the arts really cannot be counted. A few of those which were so valuable to this organization were; the practical skills, critical thinking skills, using the right side of the brain, multiple intelligence learning, income generation, understanding the historical contribution of art and the satisfaction of the process of creating.

	HANGING BOTTLE LAMP
	CANDLEHOLDER
	CHANDELIER 26" up
	CHANDELIER (12 to 20")
	CHANDELIER ((under 12")
	CONTAINER (all sizes)
	CHEESETRAY / SLUMPED BOTTLE
	DREAMCATCHER (all sizes)
	DRINKING GLASS
	FLOWER
	FLOWER VASE
	GLASS TOP TABLE

Photo credits:
Nelly Celine, Simon Magnus, Anna Dormindontova O'hagan, Alice Aida Ayers, Rachel Rockwell, Maximilliane Sale.

Special thanks to all the students, donors, sponsors, volunteers and staff of Creative Solutions Zanzibar, including; Nasra, Mabula, Mbarouk, Zawadi, Haji, Juma, Mjawiri, Magreth, Davota, Usi.

Printed in Great Britain
by Amazon